SEEING THE UNSEEN

ERIKA OKUNZUWA

A catalogue record for this work is available from the National Library of Australia

Okunzuwa, Erika (author)
The Angels Amongst Us
Seeing the unseen

ISBN 978-1-922803-09-2

Loki Regular 12/20
Cover and book design by

Green Hill Publishing

This is the true story of how I found my way back to the Lord God, the journey of my awakening.

Just before Christmas in 2019, my sons and I were abroad for a three-month vacation in the United States. We were there to see my beautiful daughter whom I hadn't seen in years, and to meet my precious grandson for the first time. We arrived just before his arrival into this world.

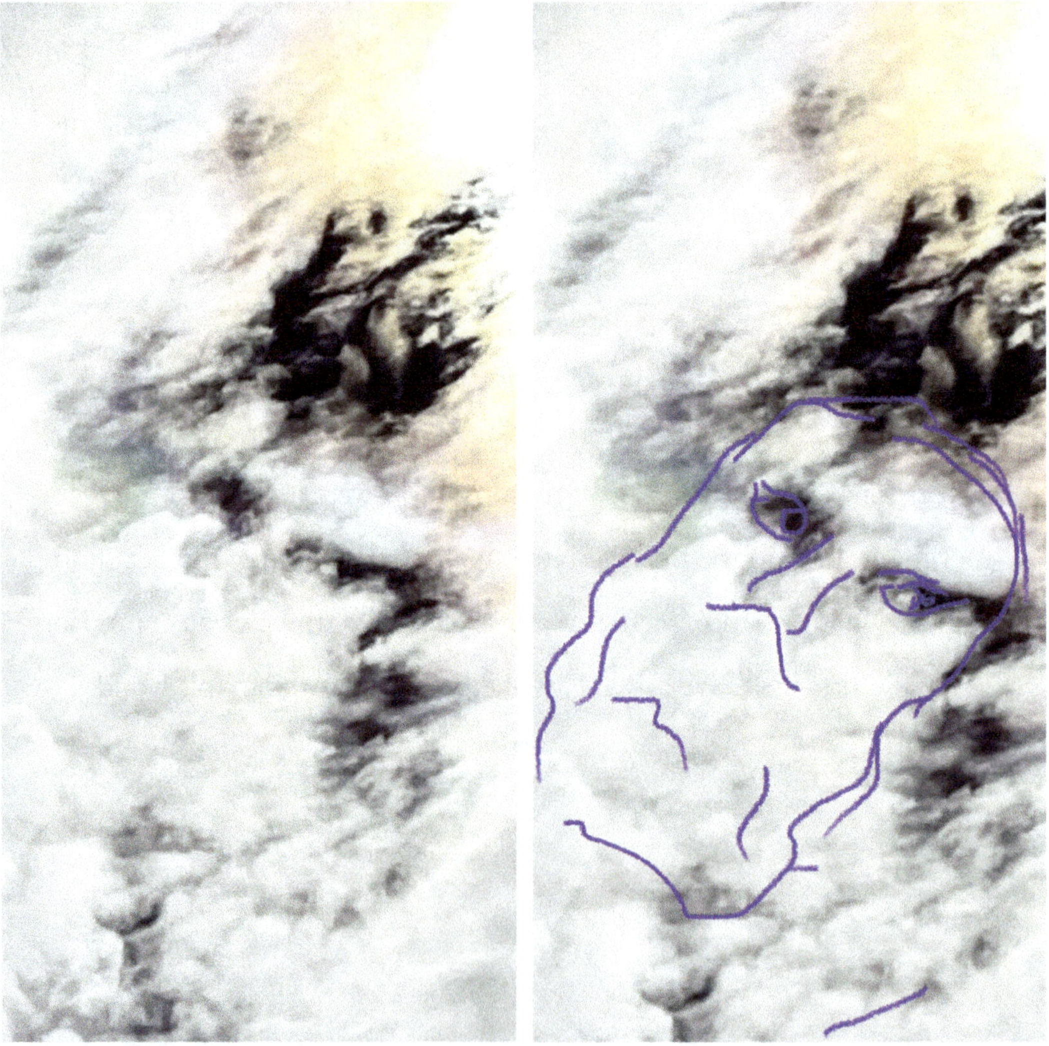

While we were there, we first heard about the pandemic, and I felt heartbroken for what was to come. I was set into a scene in which I was confused and saddened by my surroundings. Flashbacks appeared to me in which an apocalypse was about to take place in airports. How dissected and cold the crowds were, as if they were not human. All their sweetness had turned sour. *What's next?* I wondered.

I felt the desire to reconnect with our Creator as soon as I touched Australian soil. I had the feeling that I was lacking so very much, as I had been out of touch with Him, and my relationship with Him at that time was very basic. When I was reminded by my friends that I was blessed to have been away from the Australian fires and sudden pandemic tragedies, I thought to myself, *It's time to dust off the Bible.*

Erika Okunzuwa

When I got back here, I experienced a sense of being pushed,
a sense that if I could be useful and pray to the Lord,
we might be pardoned somehow. What could I do to help preserve the world?
I have no authority, and I have no say in what's coming to us,
but the power of prayer is unmatched. I prayed my heart out.
I poured out all that I had in me, for God to hear me out.
I was still lost and confused without Him.
I was searching for my true purpose in being here,
but what is our human existence without the purpose of God?
God's purpose is to give Him glory.
So I began searching for Him.

Wow! I thought to myself, *we are just vessels. We are just existing, and not living life as we used to.* It hurt me so much every time I watched a broadcast and saw the world falling apart. I thirsted for God. I craved Him. Not only that, but I was starving for every bit of knowledge about Him, and so much more. I was overthinking my worries. What would become of us?

Of course, I would never impose on the Lord by asking: *Why?* I had some sort of awareness of what needed to be done. If I repented and submitted myself, it would be a start. Maybe then the Lord would be less offended. I was overthinking. I thought that God was waiting for the last prayer to come through, and in doing that, I could comply with the Lord.

Further down the track, I realised that the Lord loves us, so why have so little faith? We are so focused on ourselves, we have failed to stay awake. We are all so absorbed by earthly elements that we are disconnected spiritually. There was so much to learn, but I was way behind. I did not have enough knowledge, so I began drilling down within myself and trying my best to come to terms with the need to stop all my transgressions.

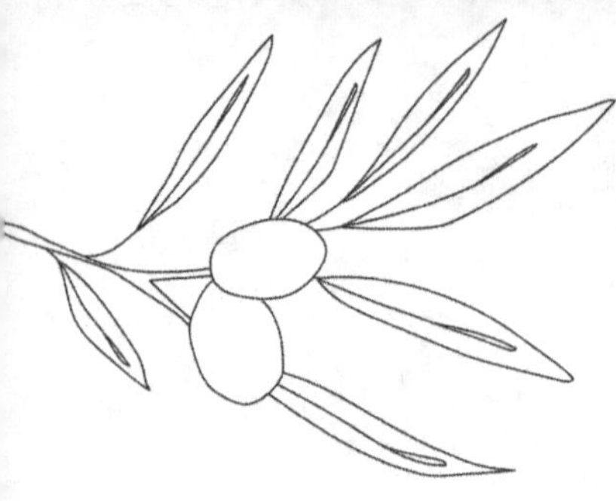

God needs us, and we need God even more.

We have the Lord's grace, and God is who we need. He is a faithful loving Father, so when he does dwell within us, and we are blessed, we are shielded by the Holy Ghost. Because we are in a transitory state, we allow ourselves to be influenced about the blessings we have gained, and we come to believe that we have done everything on our own. And then we stray and ignore the presence of the Lord. We forget how we landed here, and instead of staying connected with Him at all times, we search for him all over again. But He's cool with that.

I know for sure that nothing will hurt us when we walk with God. We think that we can navigate life all on our own, and we set ourselves on autopilot and off we go. Even though we have now picked up our mercy badge, we just repeat the depravity as soon as we fall into misery. We pursue Him only when we are down and weak. I know God is cool with this, even if we seek Him again after we have a near-death experience, are diagnosed with grievous illness, have an accident, relationship break-up and so on.

We hunt for more Wi-Fi signals and browse the latest trends more often than we seek God's accord. But when things don't go our way, we realise there is no substitute for God's plan, and we see that God loves us, no matter how many times we turn our backs on Him. So we can rest assured that God knows us as His children. We are important to God because he created us in His own image, and we are God's highest creation on earth. We need to remind ourselves that Jesus Christ died on the cross just so that he could bring us closer to God. Christ died for our sins, so that we might be forgiven.

I asked, and I prayed, and I can say I was in another element in which felt that I didn't belong on this earth. That's how mighty His Spirit is. Then I began to receive the Holy Spirit. I experienced amazing dreams almost every night. In the past, I've had many dreams and private revelations from the Lord, but it was never clear to me what should I do with them. It's possible that my eyes were tightly shut. Clearly, I wasn't equipped for what I was being shown. For sure, I was lacking in the knowledge that would help me to interpret it.

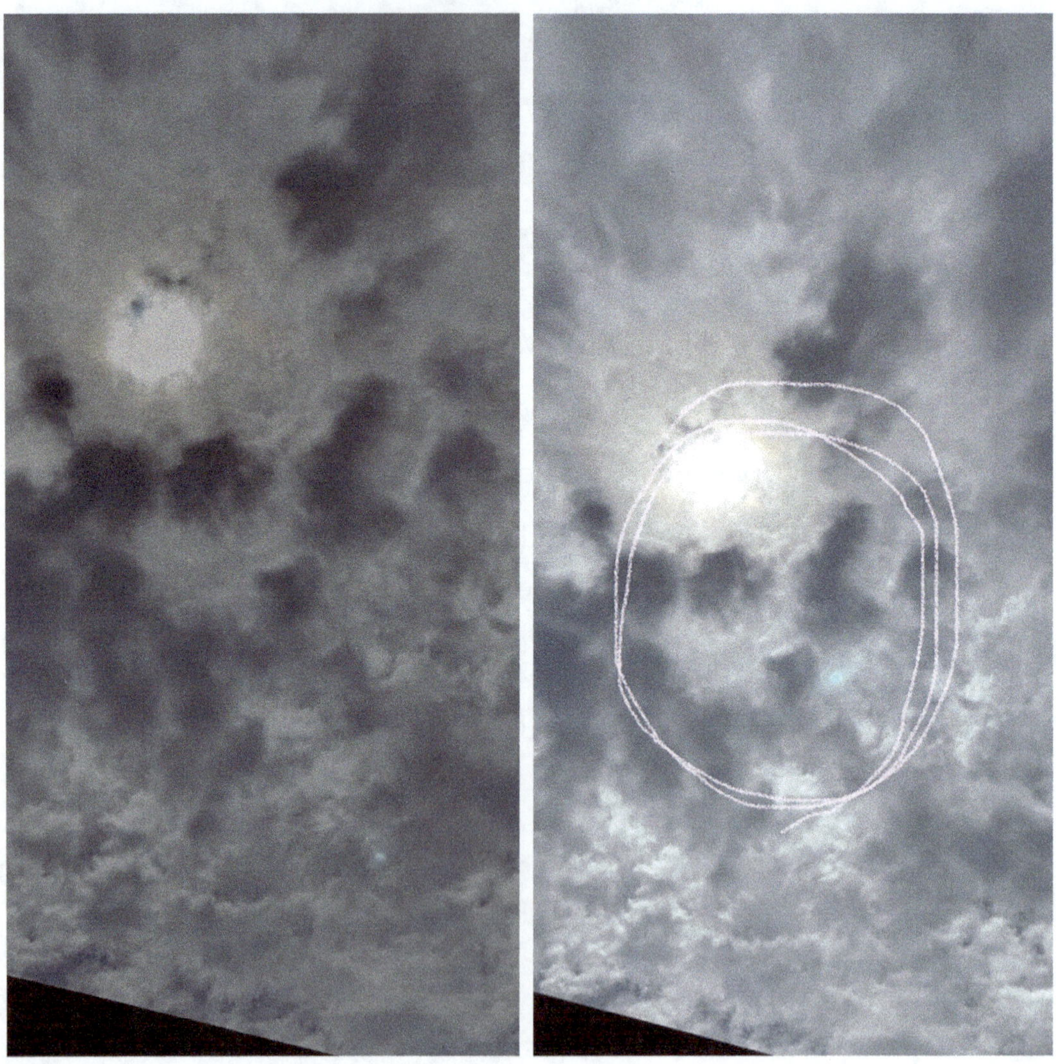

Erika Okunzuwa

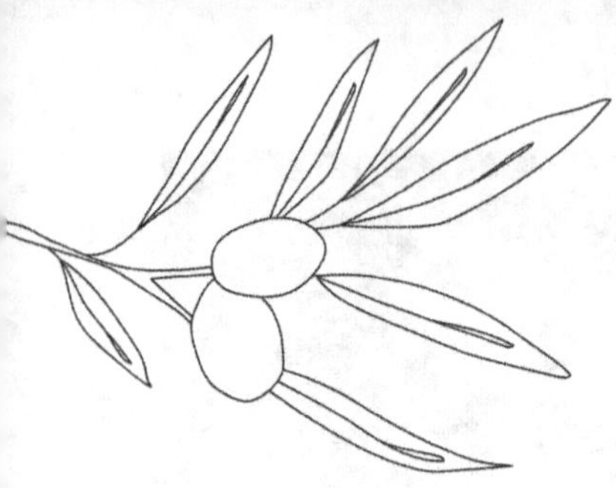

I wasn't too keen on discussing it with anyone, but I continued to sense so much, and I felt I had to be extremely cautious and sensitive about this miraculous experience. I remembered the words of Jesus when He clearly reminded us that the world hated Him first, and I understood that if I was to carry on talking about my messages from heavenly beings, I would surely be thrown aside, along with my dream notebooks; and I would be talked about as if I was not from this planet, but a creature from out of this world.

Therefore, most of the time I would note down the dreams, speaking only through my notebooks. And I kept them all this time. Then one beautiful day, I turned on the TV and was searching for nothing specific, and I randomly came across something that caught my attention. My memory was instantly jogged, and I thought to myself how inspiring it was, and how similar to something that I had witnessed a year earlier.

It was the miracle of the dancing sun. It was phenomenal.

This incident made me realise that the Lord had been speaking to me but I had not been all ears. My tears were pouring down my cheeks.

I was murmuring to my mum, *How could I have ignored and missed it all? Why did it take me a year to come to my senses? Why did I not realise sooner and toss the notebooks aside? What was I thinking?*

You are right - I wasn't thinking. Let me tell you this: if you experience what I did, please don't ignore it as I did, for it is a sign from above.
It is an eye-opener. Wake up, and pay close attention, because I know now from my own experience that God is truthful and alive. So strap on your holiness and walk with God, and you will never miss any destination. He will open your eyes and He will become their focus. Seek His presence daily.

Erika Okunzuwa

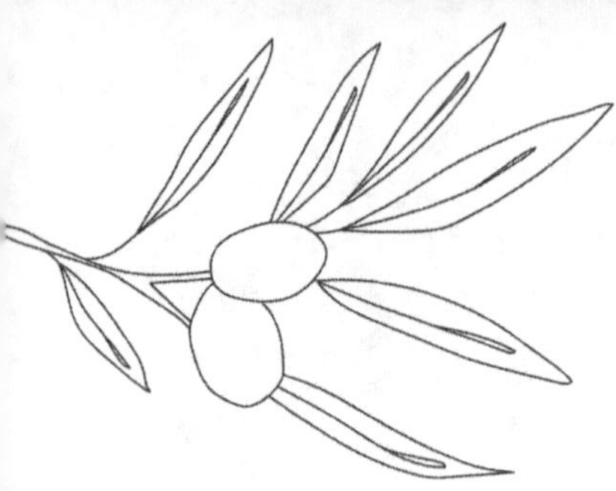

On the night that the Divine Spirit visited me, the Lord and I had a one-on-one conversation about the gifts that I have been given and how to activate them. My immediate reaction was to try to negotiate. I was saying, *But … Lord, how? Why me? You know me? … I can't talk!* I stammered. And yes, there I was in the spiritual realm, with the audacity to present myself to the Lord and backchat as if I was chatting with my kids once more.

I suggested to the Lord, *If I could be permitted to take photographs with my devices, perhaps I would be able to reveal to others that You are the Lord God and very much alive.* I addressed Him thus, and his response was pure with given with a smile. I saw before me a large crowd of people to whom I was explaining about God and His message. I don't know how I managed to do that, because in the real world of the flesh, it was as if I was a frozen statue. But the people turned their backs and walked away, and it made me so furious! Then, loudly, I called out the name of the Lord. *Lord God!* I called. And he responded and shone a dazzling light upon me, and the crowd was amazed. And then I woke.

Erika Okunzuwa

Now my eyes were open more than before. I began asking the Lord daily if I was doing what He wanted me to do. Was I praying properly? Was I aligned with Him? And so on. I had the urgent desire to tell someone, so I chose a close friend who knew the Bible inside out. She was all ears. She said that I reminded her of someone else who'd had the same experience. And she told me that this message was too beautiful not to share. I took her advice on board. But the question was: how could I be certain that I wouldn't sound delusional, and be sure that my feet were still on this planet? I was so careful about who I shared my story with. I attempted to share it with my relatives, but that did not end too well. we humans battle so much with comparing everything, and too often it leads us to envy. It's so complicated.

I was lost, but certain words kept roaming through my thoughts. I just kept asking that famous question: why is it that you can feel the wind, yet you can't see it? It is thought that seeing is believing. Right? But believing is seeing! In the same way, you may see God or you may not, but He is here. God is with you all the way, and He is omnipresent. That is why I've always been fascinated with nature, especially rainbows and animals. But I have received more blessings than I've asked for, and it just feels phenomenal.

Now, let's go deeper into my story. I am just about to reveal something, and believe me, it is not just a fluke. First, let me take you back to the story of a private revelation before any of this took place. My mum and I were about to go outside for a walk, and as we stepped outside we noticed that the sky was getting darker. We saw a large crowd of people running towards us in great fear, with immense panic on their faces. I asked my mum what was going on. Why were these people in so much distress? Their faces reminded me of famous paintings of agonised faces. I was feeling devastated. And then I looked up again, but this time from all directions a flood was coming towards us, as in the days of Noah, and it was getting closer and closer. It looked as if the people were rushing to a large glass elevator, but I wasn't paying attention to where was it going because of the distress. People were piling on top of each other. I was desperate to press the buttons, but to no avail, as my hands were shaking.

Then I was softly touched by the Holy Spirit, who was right beside me, and the Lord assured me that I did not need to do as they were doing. I was told I have the gift. And then I woke up. Gift? To this day, I have wondered what my God-given gifts are. I am still to learn about this gift, but I know it is something out of this world, for sure. I just need to figure out how to apply my God-given gift

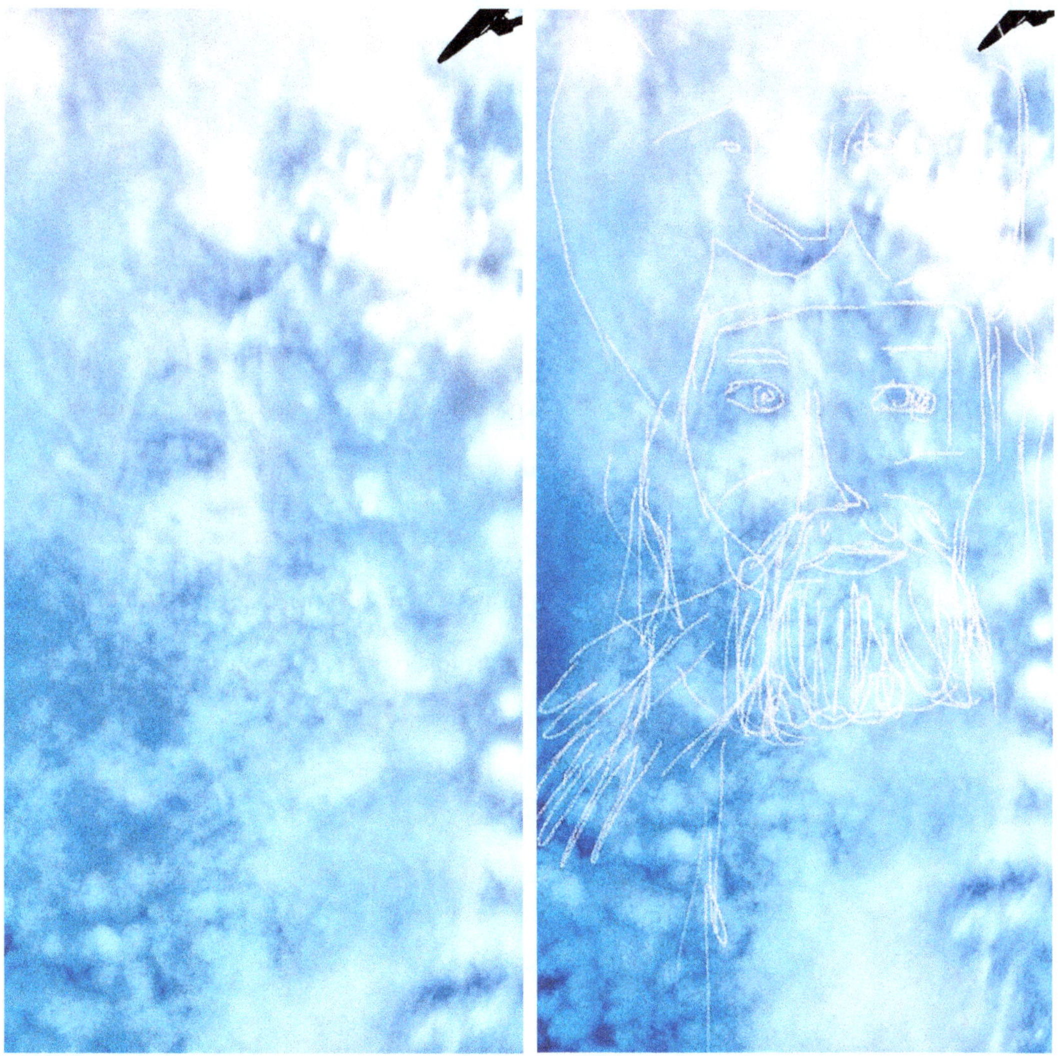

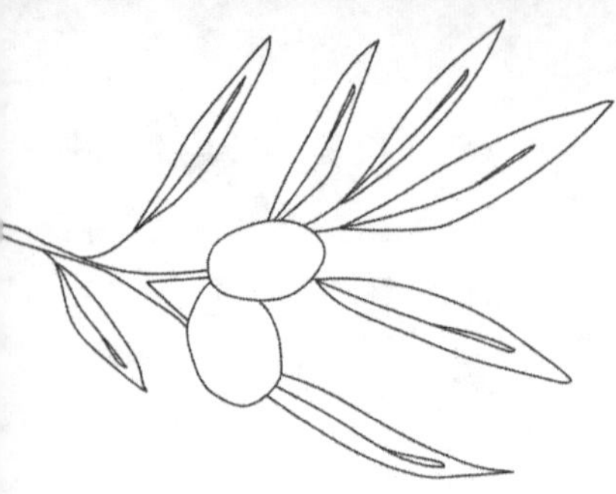

The gospel says our deepest needs reside in our hearts, not in our bodies. We must live as though our world is temporary, and eternity is our true home. *Every good gift is from above. It comes down from the Father of the heavenly lights, who does not change as the shifting shadows.* (James 1:17, King James Bible). If this is so, how is it so?

God may speak to us differently from how he may have spoken to us in the past. God speaks to us now through his Word. In the church He speaks through the priests and pastors. Study the Holy Scriptures, where He speaks to us in the voice of our heart. God also speaks through the circumstances we encounter: God so loved the world, says the Gospel. And so he speaks to us in the language of this love. He talks to us in dreams, visions, and voices. Scripture describes how God spoke directly with Elijah, Moses, Abraham, and more. They were ready to hear His voice because they simply had pure hearts.

Erika Okunzuwa

So hear my story now. I'll take you to the place of spirit versus flesh. I will bring you back to my experience of spiritual versus matter, when I chose to share my story with a local priest. My spirit was troubled after the vision of a life on earth that was about to end. I knew it wasn't an actual life, and my thoughts were pulling me down: *I am failing God, I am not working on God's deeds.*

So I came to the parish office but I couldn't see anybody there, and I left a note asking for someone to contact me when possible. We all know the power of prayer, and I was just hoping for a prayer to relieve my sadness and distress. I carried on with the rest of my day, running errands, until I received the call I was waiting for.

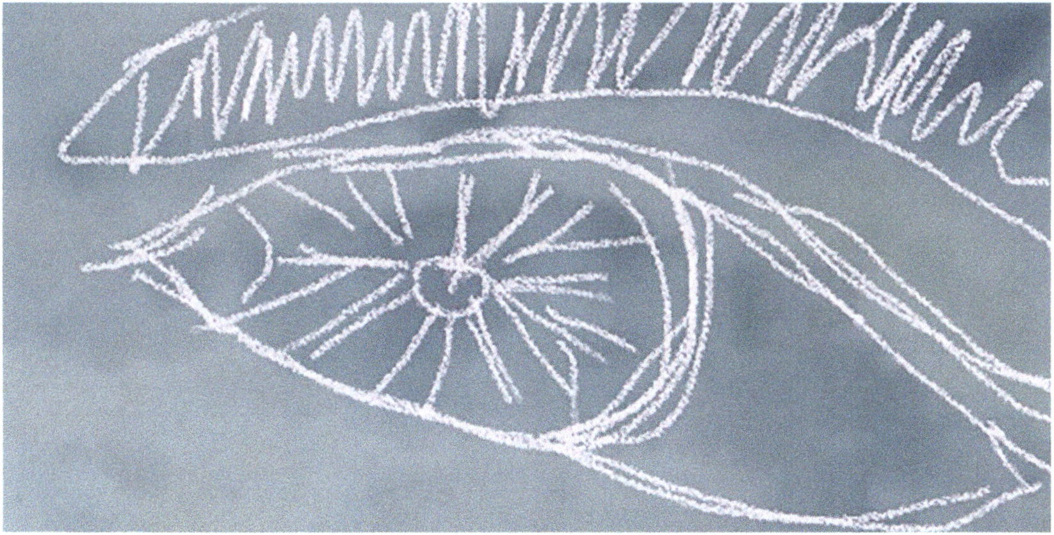

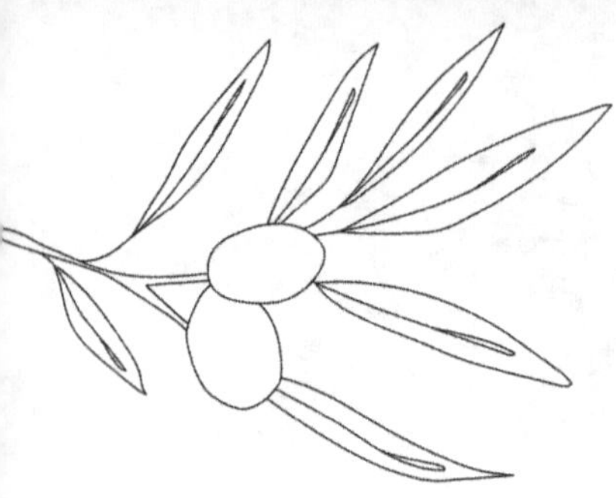

But I didn't know how to begin the discussion, as I was in a noisy place. And I was also worried, because it was about a dream. I began to express the concerns that were bothering me. I spoke of them only briefly, but he was perfectly in tune with me. When he had heard me out, his response was brief. He said with confidence that what I'd been experiencing wasn't from God. God bless his soul, but deep down I felt crushed and embarrassed. I felt that I was talking about Tinkerbell. So I politely thanked him and we ended the conversation.

My spirit was troubled and heavy on my heart because I've always been a positive person. I have always been a smiling, giggling, easy-going person, managing well under any pressure. With my friends, family and love life, all was in order. And I accepted losses, disappointments and betrayals, battling any obstacles. I felt that they were all my battles, given to me on God's timing, and that His plans were greater than mine. There is nothing that I've asked for that wasn't granted, apart from silly wishes that didn't make sense. But this was exhausting me. It forced me to the edge, and I felt a complete failure. I felt that I was ignoring my purpose in life.

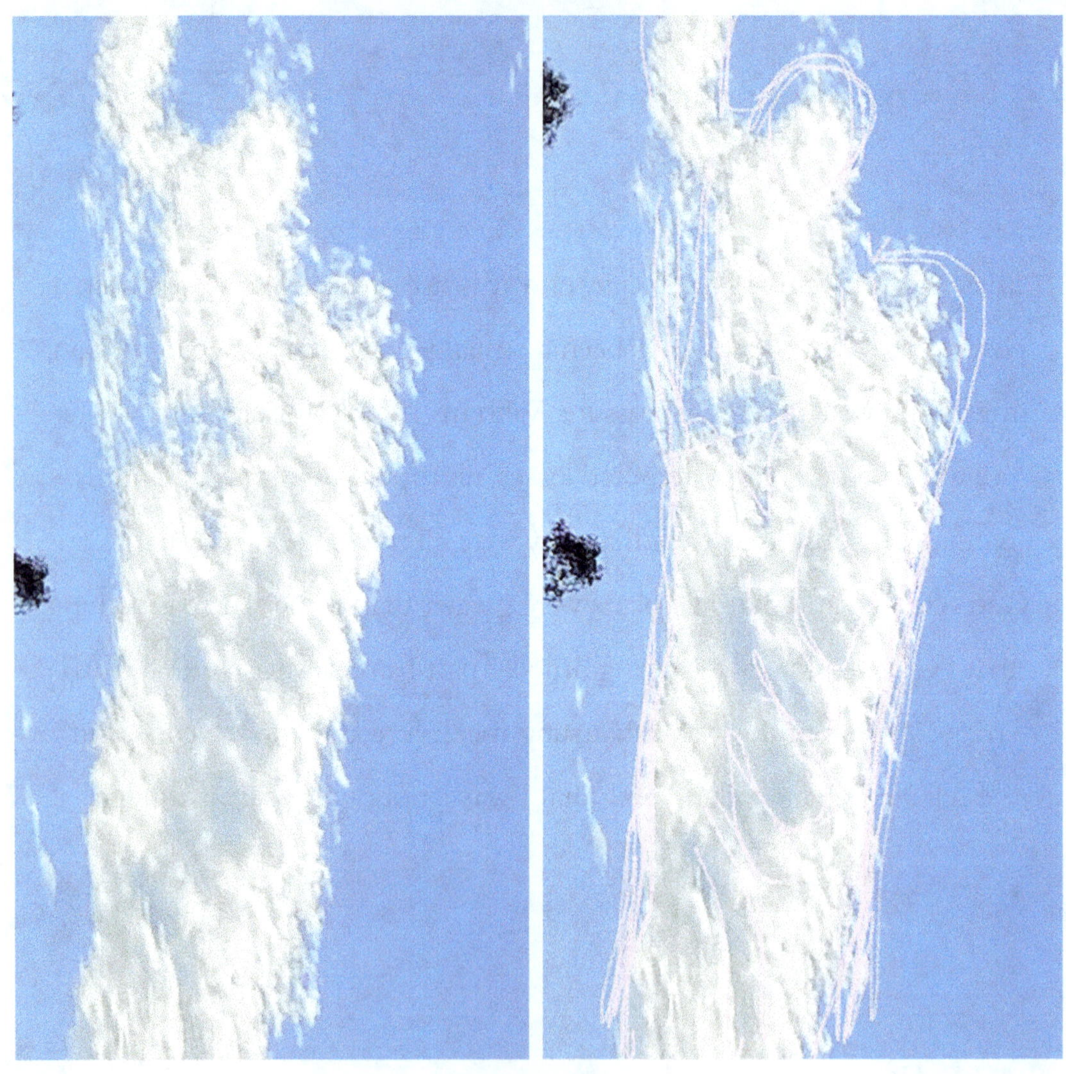

I cried for days, and then I pulled myself together and refused to allow anyone but God to navigate me with regard to my message from Holy God. The priest could not discern who had visited me. How was he able to conclude that it wasn't God whom I saw? Moses talked to a burning bush and he spoke with God. God was with Noah when he was assigned the task of building the ark. He walked with and talked to our ancestors Elijah and Abraham. And all those things were unbelievable, right? So isn't there a slight chance that he may have also walked or talked with you or me? Or any other human being? I may be unschooled, but in the eyes of the Lord I am seasoned with all his blessings, and that's all the approval I desire. My eyes are in training and I am all ears, and I refuse to accept that you cannot see the unseen or believe my testimony.

A few days after the incident with the priest, I sensed that God revealed Himself again. But this time I was wide awake. My kids and my mum and I happened to be sitting on the balcony enjoying a cool, refreshing breeze on Good Friday, and it certainly prepared us for the Lord's big reveal of signs and wonders. We were geared up with devices and all of that. Then a dark cloud covered the sunlight and a large foot shape was pointing away slightly to the right-hand side, where we were looking.

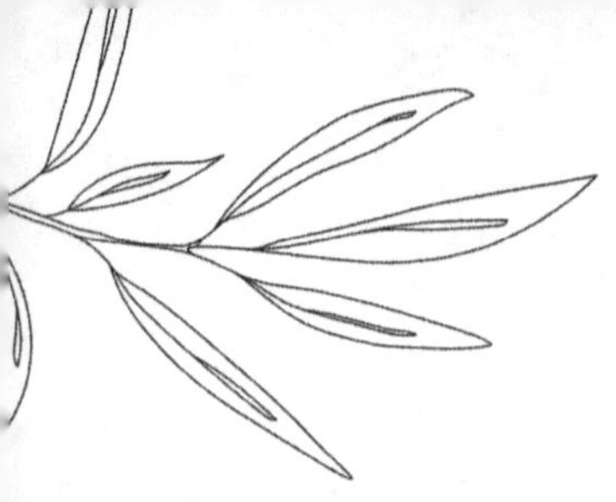

And there it was: a clear image of God's form, just as he appeared in my dreams, with long white hair and beard, and dressed in a white robe. It was phenomenal. I was shaking and crying, and all the emotions were pouring out of me. I was crying out loudly, *Oh, my God!* Then to our surprise, there was so much more - our eyes were declared open from that day on. I was so emotional. How could this be? I did not capture all of the images, and I didn't want my family to see me crying, so I bolted downstairs, and in the backyard I heard myself mumbling out words. *God! Jesus! Mother Mary!* I called. Then I looked up and there He was, only this time He was so much closer. I was so overwhelmed. I had no idea how to handle such an encounter. I knew that what I was seeing was not man made.

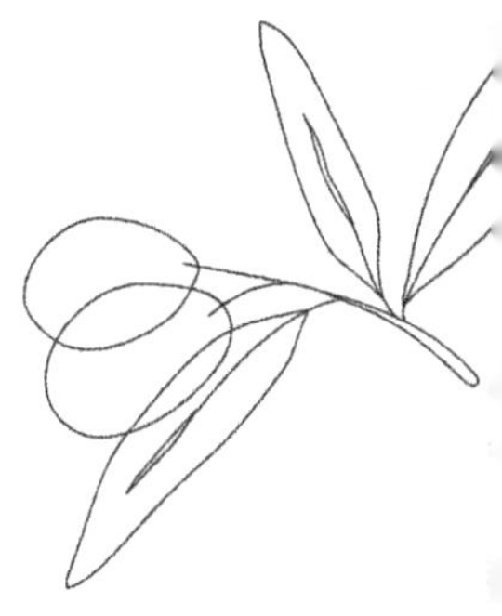

Later that night, I was too scared to scroll through my phone. I thought that maybe it had been only for my eyes to see, and the devices were unable to capture those moments. I was thinking that maybe Leonardo Da Vinci had come back to life and used the sky as a canvas to finish his masterpiece, or some such thing.

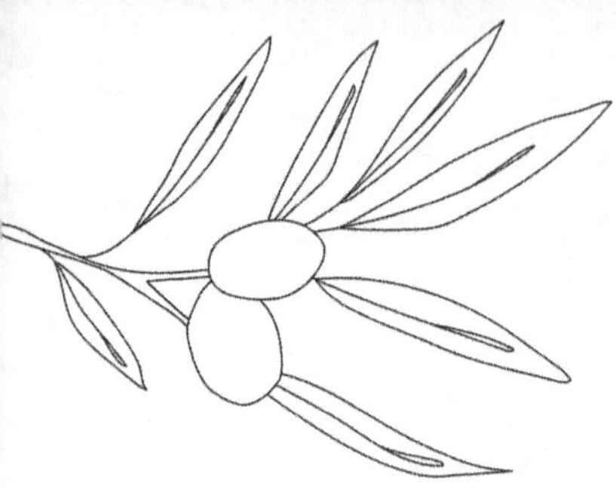

Let me summon for you this last image of these miraculous signs and happenings. When it occurred, my mum and I had our faces fixed so as not to miss a thing. We were like the sky supervisors of the month. We were caught up with gazing right through the sun, but the sunlight did not bother us, nor did it scorch us at all. It was as if there was a round metal plate in front of us. When we were looking directly into the sunlight, the best way to describe it is as a host.

And I realised that there was so much more. It was as if secret writings popped up whenever I looked directly into the sun. They were symbols that I am yet to work out. Maybe there will be a new book, if I have the privilege of decoding them. The symbols appeared like constellation signs or ancestral drawings. I don't know yet what they mean. Maybe you can help me decode them and discover their meaning. Perhaps I will show a couple of them in my next book - or perhaps I may just leave them alone.

Erika Okunzuwa

I hope you've enjoyed reading my story. I have shared it in the hope that it may inspire in you some questions about God's existence. Here is your chance to dust off your Bible, because my dream might be a sign from Jesus.

He is the way, the truth, and the life. (John 14:16)

***He is the door and through His blood,
we enter the spirit realm safely. (Ephesians 1:17-18)***

***Jesus said that no one can see the kingdom of God unless he
is born from above, born of the Spirit. (John 3:8)***

Therefore, because we have been born of the Spirit, we can see the Kingdom of God. When he says 'Seek the Kingdom of God', Jesus is telling us to interact with the Spirit world. May the Lord have mercy on us.

www.ingramcontent.com/pod-product-compliance
Lightning Source LLC
LaVergne TN
LVHW080316110826
845155LV00023B/130

* 9 7 8 1 9 2 2 8 0 3 0 9 2 *